# DOES ANYONE KNOW
# WHERE A HERMIT CRAB GOES?



Story and Pictures by MICHAEL GLASER

For Joshua and Benjamin



Library of Congress Catalog Card No. 82-84341
ISBN-13:  978-0-911635-00-3
ISBN-10:  0-911-635-00-9

Purmitt Drab was a hermit crab.

He lived at the edge of the sea.

He crawled on the ground...

...And ate what he found...

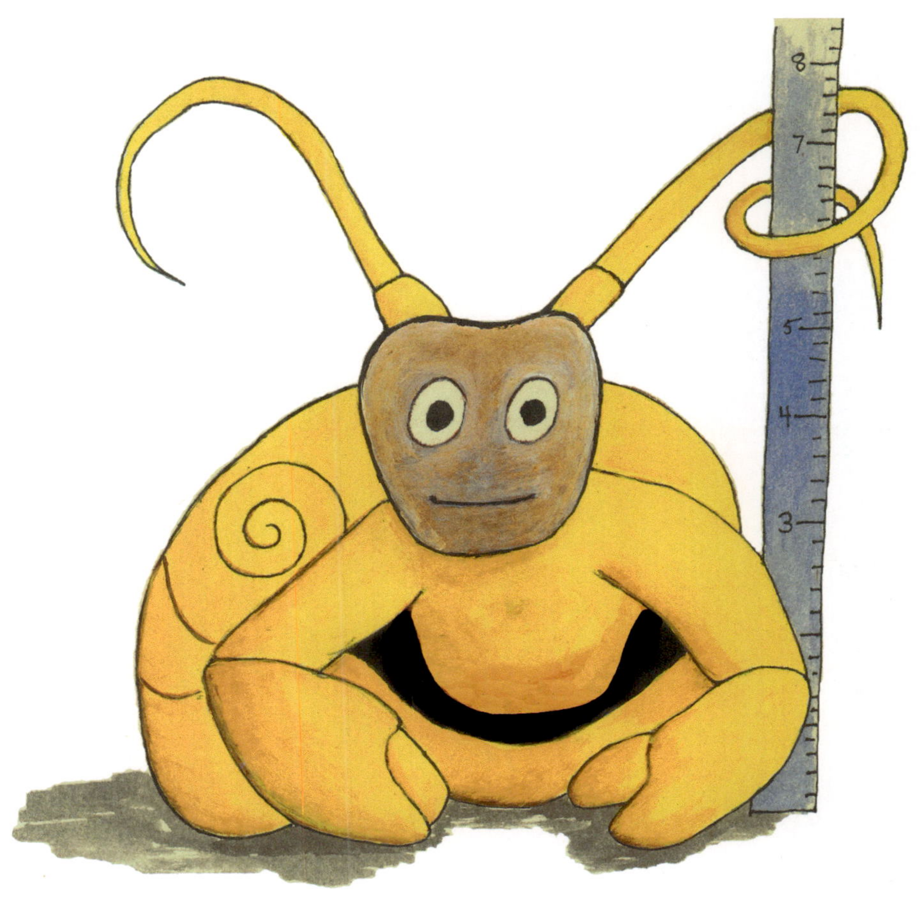

...And grew just like you and like me.

But his shell had not grown.
It wasn't his own.
He found it early last June.

It was getting too small.
There was no room at all.
He knew he would have to leave soon.

So he walked up to Sam
(Sam was a clam),
And told him he wanted to find...

A new place to go,
With more room to grow,
A  home of just the right kind.

Sam said he knew
As big as he grew,
His clamshell would grow bigger too.

"But I've heard others tell
That a hermit crab's shell
Doesn't grow as other shells do."

"Why don't you go
Where the seaweeds grow...

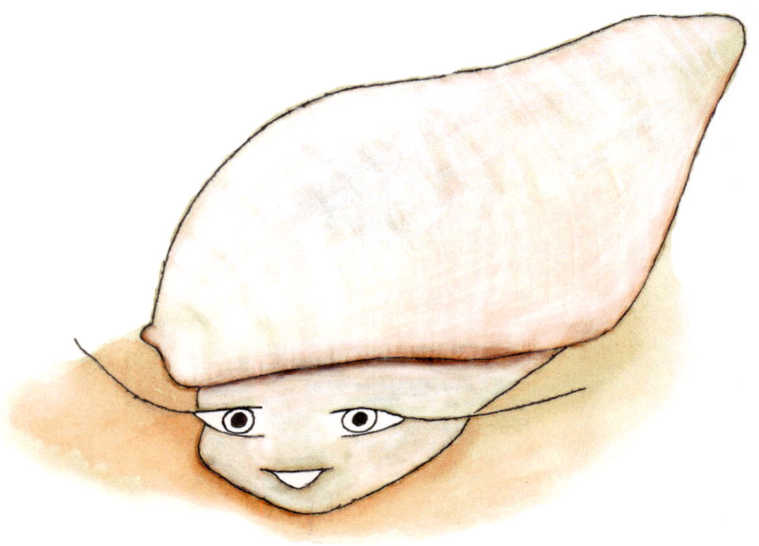

And ask Alabaster the snail?"

"Maybe she knows
Where a hermit crab goes
When he grows as big as a whale."

"I won't grow the size
Of a whale," Purmitt sighed,
"But I am growing bigger each day.
My shell is too tight.
I can't sleep at night.
So really, I must move away."

So he followed the trail
That Alabaster the snail
Had left in the sand as she crawled.

"Oh look, this trail leads
To a patch of seaweeds.
Where are you, Alabaster?" he called.

"I'm here," the snail said,
"Just over your head.
So tell me, how have you been?"

Purmit Drab cried,
"I'm getting too wide!
I need a new shell to live in."

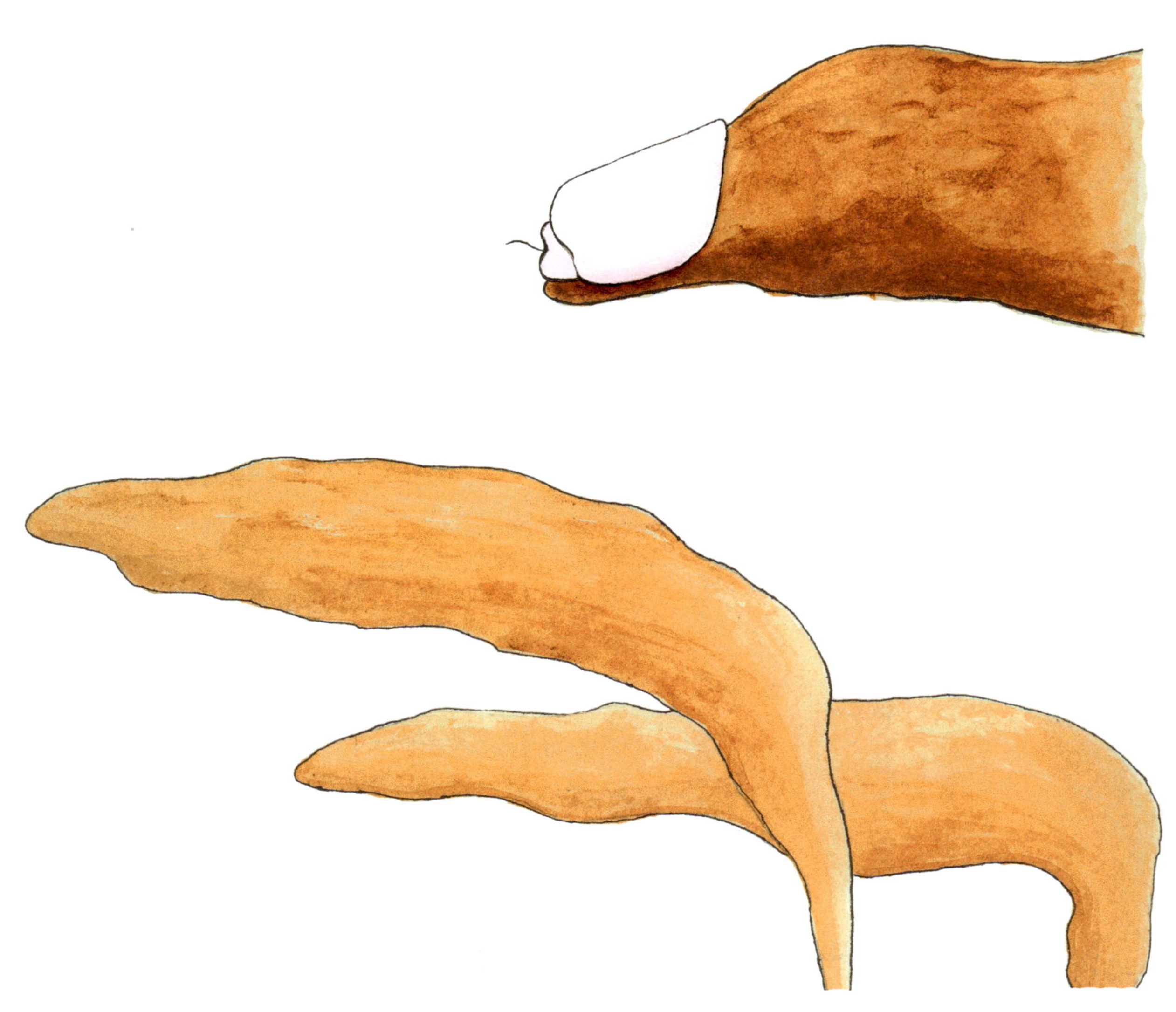

"You need a new shell?
Let me see. Well, well, well..."

"Oh yes! I have some. I do!
Right there on the ground
I have yellow and brown,
And black shells
And gray and white too!"

"At last!" Purmitt said.
"A place for my head,
And my hands and my very soft tail."

"This brown one is fine.
It's bigger than mine.
Thank you, Alabaster the snail!"

"It's time to move now.
I think I know how.
First I can put my tail in."

"And now I can slide
My whole body inside.
I did it!" he said with a grin.

"Oh look how I fit!
I can stand. I can sit.
I can roll, I can crawl, I can creep!

I can seek, I can hide.
I can stay deep inside.
I can rest, I can dream,
I can sleep!"

"I will miss, I can tell,
My old tiny shell,
But it really was too small for me.

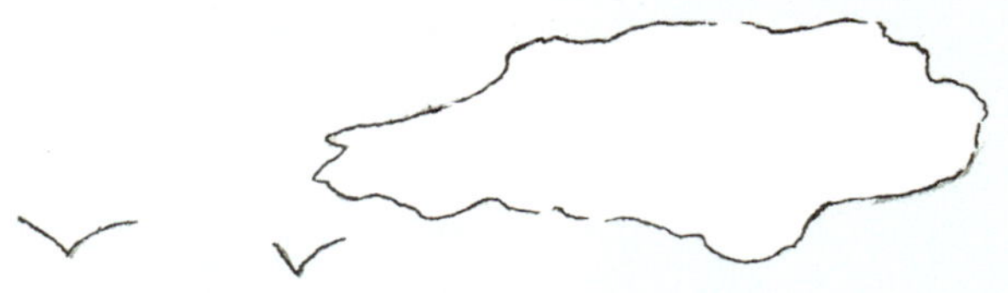

And also I know
That now I can grow
And live at the edge of the sea."

To learn more about hermit crabs, sea life, and Michael Glaser, the author
and illustrator of this book, please visit www.michaelglaser.com